HOW TO START A VENDING BUSINESS

By Antoine Cameron

Copyright and Disclaimer

No part of this book may be reproduced or transmitted in any form or by any means, mechanical or electronic, including photocopying and recording, or by any information storage and retrieval system, without permission in writing from the author (except by a reviewer, who may quote brief passages and/or short brief video clips in a review).

Disclaimer

The author makes no representations or warranties with respect to the accuracy or completeness of the contents of this work and specifically disclaims all warranties, including, without limitation, warranties for a particular purpose. No warranty may be created or extended by sales or promotional materials. The advice and strategies contained in this book may not be suitable for every situation. This work is sold with the understanding that the author is not engaged in rendering legal, accounting, or other professional services. If professional assistance is required, the services of a competent professional person should be sought. The author shall not be liable for damages arising here from. The fact that an organization or website is referred to in this book as a citation or a potential source of further information does not mean that the author endorses the information the organization or website may provide or recommendations it may make. Further, readers should be aware that Internet websites listed in this book may have changed.

Testimonials

I just wanted to write and say thank you for offering your expertise to those of us that are exploring or starting in the vending business. Your willingness to not only offer to help but also to be proactive in reaching out speaks volumes about your character. I know the time it takes to set up a website and build a newsletter. It is no small task. Your concern for my success is greatly appreciated, and I wish great times for the future for both of us. If there is ever anything I can do for you to return the favor, please just ask.

- Ron Haynes, Michigan

I just read through your book and found it very informative. Thanks for all that great advice. A lot of it I wish I had read ten years ago instead of discovering it the hard way. But that was then, and now, I am much more seasoned. I am just starting up a new route and have used PN95s in the past with good success, but I am now considering the move to vendesign 4 in 1. Thanks again for all the great information.

- Tim Holmes, Austin, Texas

Vending Success

I thank you so much for the advice I just received and the tips I got from your book. I am a college professor and I am looking to service about 30 bulk candy machines on the side for extra money. I am taking your advice, and I will buy the vending machines used with the sources you gave me. Once again, thank you.

- Matt Simpson, New York, New York

I was thinking of starting a vending business and stumbled upon your website and bought your book. Thank you for all the insight! You saved me hours of research and I have already reached out to those charities, the telemarketing service, and lined up a couple gumball machines to buy for $70–$100 each. I was originally planning on getting into pop, snacks, etc. and you brought me back down to earth. I really like your idea of peanuts and cashews in the nursing homes! I will keep you posted as to how my new fun venture is going.

- John Meyers, Chicago, Illinois

Table of Contents

How To Start a Vending Business?

"Sometimes you have to take a step backward to take a step forward."

Antoine Cameron

Why I Wrote This Book

The reason why I wrote this book was that I was tired of reading all of the so-called self-help books out there saying that they will show you the way. I am tired of buying books that claim they will show you how to buy houses with no money down without any instructions, or show you how to lose weight without exercising and just eating anything you want. All the books I have read had good information in them, but they always left me with questions on how to do this or that. That is why I wrote The Gumball Guru Vending Course because I wanted to give people a step-by-step guide that they could read and then go out and be successful. I wanted to show people that there is another way to make money instead of going to work living from paycheck to paycheck. I want to show people that there is a way to get out of the rat race and that you do not need a lot of money or time to start. If you are looking for a way to make an extra couple thousand dollars a month by working one or two days a month, then this book is for you. If you already found a better way, let me know. Also, if you have any questions about bulk vending, or if I left anything out, please let me know at antoinecameron@gmail.com

A Little Background

It was March 24, 2003, and I was getting ready to go to the ballpark. This was my third minor league spring training with the Chicago Cubs. I woke up my roommate at 6:00 a.m., and we headed down to the clubhouse. Things were not looking good for me. I spoke with my agent a week before about my situation, and I told him I did not think there was a future for me with the Chicago Cubs. He told me to hang in there and see how things played out. At that time, I was batting .363 for the spring, and the year before that, I was an all-star, but that does not mean anything in pro ball. We got to the park, and we got suited up as usual and headed out to the field to stretch. We were playing at home against the Padres, and I was happy, because I did not have to travel. After doing our usual batting practice and field drills, we went back into the locker room to change into our game uniforms. While I was taking off my practice jersey, my coach said the farm director wanted to see me. I knew I was not going to be released because the farm director releases players in the morning. So, I went into his office to see him. He told me that I have been traded to the Texas Rangers. Just like that, my career with the Chicago Cubs was over. I packed up my bags and told all my friends that I would see them in the big leagues. Little did I know seven days later I would also be released from the Texas Rangers. My baseball career was over. I came up short. I never saw one day in the big leagues. What was I going to do now? Not only did I get released from baseball, but also six months later, my wife left me and took our two kids and the one she was carrying with her. You want to talk about your life turning upside down, well mine was, but I was determined to make it.

It was September 2003 and I found a bottling company to work for. It was a good job with benefits. My salary was 40,000 a year there, and our schedule was pretty cool. I would work four days and then have four days off. They were 12-hour shifts, but I did not care. All I cared about was my four days off. I was pretty good at what I did there, but it was not baseball, so I was miserable of course. Well anyway, the wife was long gone by now, and she was not coming back. She already had a new boyfriend, which puzzled me because she was pregnant and had two kids, but you never know these days. Anyway, I was making decent money paying the bills, but I knew my divorce was coming up, and child support would soon be on the way, so I knew I needed to make some extra money somehow someway, and getting a second job was out of the question for me. I loved my four days off, and I was not going to screw them up with a second job.

I tried everything from trying to buy real estate with no money down, to multi-marketing companies: prepaid legal, world leadership group, molecular, Herb life, and Amway. Yes, I tried them all without much success. I tried selling items on eBay, which I had success with, but when I ran out of things to sell, I was out of business. I tried to find drop shippers, these are companies you do not have to buy anything up front from; when your item sells on eBay, you just send them the money, and then, they ship it to your customer. The only problem with those companies was their prices were not low enough for me to make a profit on eBay. So, I was still searching for something I could do to make some money on the side. But the way I wanted to make money had to have some key ingredients. It could not cost much to start because I was broke, it could not take a lot of my time, or I might as well just go out and get another job, and I did not want to have to depend on anybody else for my success like those multi-marketing companies telling you to invite all of your family and friends to those freaking meetings. By this time of my life, I was the laughing stock of the family. I was that crazy guy that would try anything to make money. I was just about to give up and just work for the next 45 years of my life and retire when I was searching franchises one day on the Internet and discovered a company called Candy King. At first glance, I thought to myself, "bulk vending machines? How much money could be made in that?" Then I kept reading, and they had the profit calculator on the webpage. The website said that bulk vending machines, on average, range from $2.00–$3.00 a day in sales, which at the time did not seem outrageous. On the low side, $2.00 a day for one machine equaled $60 a month. If I had 20 of these candy machines, I could be making $1,200 a month gross. I found the answer to my prayers. Sign me up.

After about a month of investigating this bulk vending business and doing a lot of research on the Internet, I called my brother and told him I was going to try and make some money in this bulk vending business that I found. He immediately laughed at me and said, "What, those machines you see at the stores and pizza parlors?" He then said,

"What are you going to do, go around picking up quarters? That's Chump Change." And then, he laughed again. We hung up the phone, but I was not deterred by his comments. I knew I was on to something, and I wanted to prove to my brother and everybody else that I could make this bulk vending business work.

"Find a job you like and you add five days to every week."

H. Jackson Brown Jr.

My First Machines

After going over the Candy King website, I got to the contact number and made a call to the company. I was very excited. I talked to one of the sales representatives, and he sent me out a brochure of the machines and how much they cost. I got the package the next day, and I was very disappointed to see how much they were selling these machines for. They wanted $16,000 for 20 machines. That was way out of my price range. I only had $1,500 to spend and that was barely going to buy three machines. The sales representative also informed me that they do not sell anything less than 20 machines, so I was back to square one. I decided to do a search on eBay just to see what came up, so I typed in "Candy King vending machines," and a whole bunch of machines came up. They were all $150 and under. I almost hit the floor when I saw the bargain basement prices they were selling on eBay. And to think that if I had $16,000 lying around, I would have probably bought the machines from Candy King. I looked at some of the sellers, and I found a guy in Florida who was in the army who said that his wife was tired of the business and that she wanted him to sell all of the machines they had. He had 14 machines, and he said he would sell them to me for $1,300 including shipping. Since I live in California, I got a great deal. I got my vending machines the next couple of weeks, and I was excited. I thought I was on my way, but boy, did I have a lot to learn, from finding locations to what kind of candy to use. The Candy King machines I bought had three candy heads on them. This means I could put three different kinds of candy in them. But really, I could only put two different kinds of candy in them because the middle one was fixed to use only 1-inch gumballs, or 1-inch bouncing balls. So, I pondered: what should I put in my first machines? I read and read on the Internet and found that peanut M&Ms were one of the top-selling candies. But they were chocolate, and I did not want the hassle of cleaning my machines of melted chocolate. So, I decided to go with the 1-inch gumballs in the middle. I also chose Mike 'n Ikes and Skittles. I did not buy any Runts or any other cheap candy that these websites tried to sell you and convince you that you will make money buying that crap. I mean, seriously, when was the last time you went to the store and bought a bag of Runts? So, I ran down to Sam's Club and bought a box of gumballs which were $15 and two bags of Mike 'n Ikes which was over $11 and two bags of Skittles which were over $11. Man, candy was expensive. It cost $37 to fill up the machine, and when the machine emptied out, I would have over $280 in quarters. This is the kind of profit margins I was looking for. If I could buy something for $40 and sell it for $280 bucks on eBay, I would be a rich man. So, I took my candy home and filled up my first machine. I ran through my house and searched for a quarter to put in the machine. I found a couple of quarters and put them into the machine. I turned the knob, and presto, candy came out. I was really excited about the vending machine business now, and I could not sleep. The next day, I picked up my kids and brought them to my house for the weekend. I did not tell them that I was going into the vending machine business; I wanted them to be surprised. I parked my car in the garage door, and then I let them go in the house before me. I had the machines in the living room. When they saw the machines, they went crazy and told me, "Daddy, give me a quarter." I gladly gave them a quarter and then watched them put their little hands in the machine and get the candy out. I was further convinced that I made the right decision on going into the candy business. Now, my only dilemma was where I was going to put my 14 machines.

My First Couple of Locations

I remember it like it was yesterday: I was doing another search on the Internet about how to secure locations for my candy machines. There were basically two kinds of ways to find locations: go around knocking on doors or calling yourself to find locations, or pay someone to find them for you. At first, I listened to my dad. He said I needed to get out there and beat the doors down and find locations myself. So, I did. I made calls, talked to local businesses in my area, and with no luck, I did not get one machine placed. My dad went out to prove me wrong, and within one day, he got one of my machines placed at a Goodyear dealership in Chino Hills, California. He gave me the contact info, and I ran over there and placed my machine. I put it in the corner like the manager of the shop wanted. I worked less than two miles from the place, so checking on it would be no problem. I got two more machines placed at my brother's job. He worked at a car dealership. I went and talked to the service manager who wanted a machine placed. He wanted a machine in the service area and in the break room. So, I was happy that he wanted two machines instead of the one I had anticipated on placing. So, I had three machines placed so far, but I wanted to try a locating service and see what kind of locations they could get me. They were a telemarketing locating service. I gave them a couple of zip codes, and they would call businesses and try to get my machines placed. It cost $50 a machine to get them placed, so I tried them out and paid for two locations, which cost me $100. Within a week, they found two locations for me: one at a realty business, and the other at a nursing home in the employees' break room. I did not think too much of these locations, but hey, I was not making any money with these machines in my house, so I decided to give these locations a try. I promised myself I would wait a month until I checked my first five machines. I was hoping to pick up $300 gross according to my calculations with five machines. Or so I thought.

"Aerodynamically, the bumble bee shouldn't be able to fly, but the bumble bee doesn't know it so it goes on flying anyway."

Mary Kay Ash

My First Time Picking Up Quarters

A month passed and it was my first time going to my machines. I was excited because I knew I was about to pick up about $300, and it was going to be a great weekend. The first machine I went to was the Goodyear dealership, the location my dad secured for me. I ran in there, and I was kind of puzzled. It looked like the vending machine had not even been touched. I stood there for a moment and then proceeded to the machine. I got my key out and turned the machine around and opened the back where the money was. I got my little bag out and started grabbing the quarters. There was a decent amount of quarters there; not what I was expecting, but I would not know the real truth until I got to the car and counted them. I locked the vending machine back up, said goodbye to the manager, and proceeded to my car to count the quarters. I took the quarters out of the bag and counted them. When I got to the end, I had $15 in quarters. It was a small cry from the $60 I thought I was going to pick up. I was a little disappointed, but hey, how long did it take me to make $15 in two minutes? So I could not complain. I drove to my next location: the old folk's home, which is close to mine. I went into the break room, and the same thing happened: the candy machine looked like no one bought anything. I turned the machine around and found only $5.00 in quarters. Now I was really mad. I should have at least $120 in my pocket by now, and I only got 20. Even though I was not getting the money I thought I would be getting on my vending machines, it was still fun and exciting, so I trekked on. The next location I went to was the realty place. Before I got out of the car, I already prepared myself for the worst. I walked up the stairs and opened the door to the realty office when, to my surprise, there was a significant amount of candy missing from the machine. I tried to keep my composure, but I could not; I was too excited. I walked quickly over to the machine and opened the back side of the machine. There were so many quarters in the machine; they were stacked on top of each other. It took me about five minutes to get all of the quarters out of the machine. I was thinking to myself, this is why I got into the business. I smiled at the receptionist as I left and then quickly hurried to my car to count my quarters. I counted $40 in quarters. Now, I was thinking to myself, this is what I am talking about. This is why I got into the business. I hurried to my other location, my brother's job, the car dealership, which I picked up $25 each from both machines. So, in about an hour, I picked up $110. It was not the $300 I thought I was going to pick up, but the $110 was not that bad. I then knew when I got home that I had something great. I just had to work a little bit harder. It came to me as a no-brainer: the more machines I had out there working for me, the more money I could make. I wanted to write this little brief biography of my first machines because I wanted you to know where I started from to where I am today. I started with 14 machines; now I have 312. The first time I went to pick up money from my machines, I collected a little bit over $110. Today, I pick up a little bit over $7,500 month after month after month, working 24 hours a month (if you call it work), but that is all the time I devote to the business. I know what you are saying: "That is great, but how can I do that?" Do not worry, I am going to tell you everything I know about vending, from where I got my machines, to what candy I used in almost 90% of my machines, to how I find locations, to setting up the machine, and to setting the candy wheels to dispense just the right amount of candy so your customers do not feel cheated, and you are still making a high profit. I will tell you about charities and give you a list of the ones I use. I will also tell you why I believe that this business is a passive income and this is the gateway to financial freedom, getting out of the rat race and stop living from paycheck to paycheck.

Is Bulk Vending Really a Passive Income?

If you own five apartment buildings and you are bringing in $25,000 a month making a couple of calls and checking on your management company every now and then, I guess that is pretty passive. Or if you are good at recruiting people and you recruited a couple of hundred people and your down line is growing and everybody is participating in the multilevel marketing program that you are in, then I guess going around picking up quarters is probably a lot of work. But for most of us who do not have the money, credit, or resources to invest in real estate, or the time to convince people and sell them on a multilevel marketing company, then bulk vending might be an excellent business for you. If you do not know what passive income is, the definition is that once you set something up, money comes in month after month with no more work involved, or with very little upkeep. That is why passive income is so powerful: it gives you freedom and time to do the things you really want to do. I always ask people in my family, if they could make an extra $1,000 maybe $2,000 a month, would it change their lives? You bet it would. Ask yourself the same question. What if you could add another $2,000 a month to your salary right now, without any more work than you are doing right now? You would probably see the world a little bit different. Maybe you would buy a new car or go on that vacation you have been putting off the last five years, because you could not afford it. Or maybe just the peace of mind that you know that you have all the bills covered and a little extra left over. Well that is what I thought when I started in this bulk vending business. That is the great thing about passive income and the bulk vending business. Once you got it set up and running, all you have to do is maintain it, and the money comes in month after month with very little effort. And the best part is, once you put money in the business, you do not have to add new money to the business. For example, let us say you are starting out, and you want to buy one machine. Say, the machine cost $150, and you go out and buy some candy to fill it up which is $50, and you pay someone to find you a location which is another $50. So, it cost you $250 to get your one vending machine candy and a location. But this is the best part: you are done paying out of your pocket now. The candy machine will pay for itself now. You do not have to put any new money in the vending machine. So, after the first month, you get $40 out of the machine. If you have it set upright, 70% of the money should be profit – which I will show you in later chapters – you should profit about $28, so you save the other $12 for candy. So, in four months, you have enough money to buy new candy which will be about the time you need to replace the candy. Did you put any new money in the business? No. Did you calculate how long it took you to recoup your $250 a month, which really does not matter because you are bringing in $28 every month for as long as you have the location? Do you see the power of these machines? What if you had 20 of these machines, or 50? Let me tell you right now, bulk vending is a numbers game: the more machines you have, the more money you are going to make.

"If you don't like something, change it. If you can't change it, change your attitude. Don't Complain."

Maya Angelou

Why Bulk Vending?

What other business can you make 70 percent profit and not have any special contacts to wholesalers and middle men? All you need is a Costco or Sam's Club card and you are in. That is where I buy my candy and still buy my candy. The most important reason why bulk vending is way to go is time. It does not take a lot of your time to run a route. I only devote 24 hours a month on my business, and I collect over $7,500. How do you like that as passive? Work 24 hours at your job and tell them to write you a check for seven grand? Yes, I know, good luck.

You might be thinking, what about those big vending machines that dispense soda, chips, cookies, and candy bars? Those machines must make a lot of money, and they do, but that is a job. You have to work a route like that every week. Do you know how much one of those machines cost? A lot of money; we are talking thousands here for one new machine. And the upkeep there is a lot of maintenance with these big soda and snack machines. You also have to have a truck or van and some strength to move these machines. What happens when the location does not want the soda machine anymore? A big problem; now, you have to go down there and pick up the machine and find another location for it. If you pay someone to find you another location, it is going to cost you $300 plus, and you have to place the machine yourself. I hope you are really strong and you have a big truck. If you are running a bulk vending route and the owner says he does not want the machine anymore (believe me, it happens), all you do is say "ok" and put the machines in the back of your car. No problem. I do not have to come back and schedule a time to pick up the machine or rent a van or a moving company. You also need a license to have soda and snack machines on locations. In most states, for bulk, you do not need anything. If you are interested in the soda and snack machines, I know of a guy who wrote an e-book on his business. He has some great ideas, and he tells you how to get free soda machines via being a third-party vendor. This means Pepsi and Coca-Cola will give you a brand new machine and set it up for you, and all you have to do is buy the soda direct from them and keep it filled up. You keep all the money, and they take care of the machine, doing any repairs needed. Sounds like a great idea, right? Well it is, but it is not as easy to be a third-party vendor as Rob states in his book. You better know what you are doing because Pepsi or Coca-Cola will test your knowledge in vending. Before I decided to go into bulk vending, I checked into third-party vending. After making a couple of calls for about a week, I finally got a contact into the third-party vending program with Pepsi. Look and behold, the guy went to my high school, he knew me, but I did not know him. He said he knew me because of baseball. We had a short conversation about the good ole days, but then, he said he was not in the third-party vending department anymore, so he gave me a number of a lady who was. She was tough. First of all, you had to buy the soda from them, at least four cases a week. Next, they did not deliver the Pepsi to your house anymore (at least in my area), so you had to have a physical business address that they could deliver it to. My uncle had a little warehouse in Ontario, California, that I asked him if I could use because I needed an address; anyway, I could just put the soda in my car when Pepsi will deliver it, so I had that covered. Then the lady told me that I needed 20 locations up front, and they had to be good locations. I also needed around 70 employees. And oh, did I forget to tell you that they only supplied the soda machines? What about the snack machines? You had to get those on your own. So, you had to come up with 20 snack machines, and you had to fill them up with chips and candy bars. Also, you had to find 20 good locations (and she was picky, remember); I was not good at finding locations, and I did not have an extra $50,000 around to buy 20 snack machines. So, I forgot about vending with soda and snack machines. If I have an extra $50,000 lying around, I would buy bulk vending machines.

Vending Machine Scams

Vending scams are everywhere, on the Internet and in your local paper. They always offer big dreams and promises. They always paint the picture of you sitting on the beach having a drink and playing golf. We all have seen this type of advertising in some way, form of fashion. Just do not fall for it.

Typical Scam

The typical scam looks something like this: someone representing the company, rents a hall of some sort, and holds a meeting. You probably got an invitation to a meeting like this in the mail, and it seems like a good opportunity. You show up and there is a big show and dance number, and they get you all excited. Then, they want $10,000 for 20 machines with no locations or candy. Do not get me wrong; you will get the vending machines you purchased, but you have overpaid dearly. Five hundred dollars per machine is not the way to start your vending business.

Stay Away from Vending Machine Scams

If you get this kind of message in the mail, throw it away. Vending is a great business, and you do not need $10,000 to start. A couple hundred bucks are all you need to get one machine, some candy, and a location. Do not be suckered into these scams.

"There is no such thing as a long piece of work, except one that you dare not start."

Charles Baudelaire

How To Get Started

First and foremost, with anything you do, you have to have some goals. You have to have short-term goals and long-term goals. It is so important to write these goals down on paper. Put them on the fridge and let everybody see them. This is so powerful. It will make you accountable, and it will keep you on course and focused. Here is a quick example of how goal-making works: let us say you want to make $1,000 a month in your vending business in the next year. So, when month 12 comes around in your vending business, you want to make $1,000 a month. That is something to be proud of, right? That would be something to talk about. Well, how many machines do you need to make $1,000 a month? If you do it my way, you are going to need 50 vending machines. Remember, $20 a month profit is what I get from my machines. So, $20 × 50 = $1,000. You might be thinking, man, that is a lot of machines, I cannot do that. Well, let us break these 50 machines down into smaller goals. Remember, our goal is for our business to be making at least $1,000 a month in a year, so we know we need at least 50 machines to make this happen. Let us divide 50 by 12, and we get 4.167. So, all you have to do is get four machines placed per month. Now anybody can do that, right? That sounds a lot easier than 50 machines. Just concentrate on getting four machines filled and on location per month, and in 12 months, you will be at your $1,000 dollar a month goal. Sounds easy enough, and it is when you set goals and break them down into smaller tasks.

Choosing Your Vending Machine

Research Your Machine

Picking the right vending machine for your business is very important. There are a couple of things you need to know about vending machines, and I will explain them in this chapter. First, all vending machines are not created equal. There are plenty of people out there who say the type of vending machine does not matter, but it does. You want this business to be as easy as possible, and choosing the wrong vending machine can put you out of business. When you choose a machine, there are some key things that you will want to have, and those are interchangeable canisters, steel coin mechanisms, and hopefully, a steel case. These types of machines will give you a lot less headache, and you will be glad you took my advice.

Interchangeable Canisters

Interchangeable canisters can be separately removed from the machines. For example, let us say you have a three-head bulk vending machine, and you need to change the Skittles since they are getting low. You arrive on location, you open the machine, and you pull off the canister that is holding the Skittles. You take it back to your car and put new candy in it, or you load it up right there on the spot. If you do not have these interchangeable canisters, it would be impossible to do this. You would have to dig out the old candy by hand, and it is virtually impossible to get out all the old candies and replace it with new candies. It also takes a long time. I want to say this again, these interchangeable canisters are a must-have with any vending machine you buy, or you will be sorry. Those of you out there who have three- or four-head machines that do not have interchangeable canisters know how hard it is to change the candy out of them. You certainly cannot change candy on location.

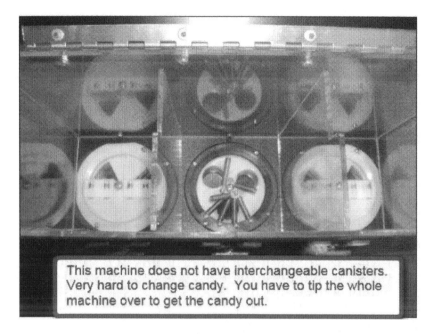

This machine does not have interchangeable canisters. Very hard to change candy. You have to tip the whole machine over to get the candy out.

Coin Mechanisms

The second most important thing for your vending machine is the coin mechanism. I am always surprised when I go service my route and I see so many machines that have plastic coin mechanisms. People, this is only going to make your job hard if you buy machines with plastic coin mechanisms. Can you run a vending route with plastic coin mechanisms? Sure, but you better have spare parts and prepare for your machines to get jammed.

Save yourself a lot of headache and buy a machine that has metal coin mechanisms.

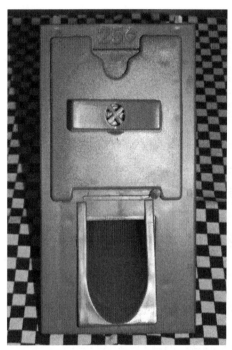

This is a picture of a plastic coin mechanism. I would avoid these like the plague. My friend has over 300 of these machines on route, and he does very well. It can be done, but just be prepared and have back-up parts. Vendstar Machines are probably the easiest machines to get and find, so just be prepared to do a little extra work with these machines.

You Want a Vending Machine with a Small Footprint

This machine has a one foot imprint very good takes up very little space

The machine above has a very small imprint, and this is exactly what you want when you decide on what vending machine to buy. A small footprint is a bulk vending machine that does not take up more than two feet of space on the floor. You do not want your machine taking up more than two feet of space on the floor because it will be hard to place the machine, and if you use a locating service, then they are going to charge you more.

Buy Machines that Are Mostly Metal

The picture above is one of my first vending machines when I started out. I just thought any machine would be okay. Boy was I wrong. Look at the arrows: after about four months on location, the bottom started cracking, the machine was unstable, and I had to take it home. The sides were cracking as well, and candy was falling outside. I do not know if it was because of the heat (I live in California) or just a poorly designed machine. But after a while, all of my machines, like the one above, went the same, and I had to replace them.

Now, look at my Vendesign Machine – all metal and no problems. I have had these machines for about five years now and have not had one problem with them. I never carry any tools or extra parts. I believe these machines are the best.

Does Your Machine Hold Gumballs?

Please do not assume that your vending machine holds 1-inch gumballs. This is a big mistake that a lot of people make, including me. Gumballs are, by far, the most profitable item you can put in your vending machine. I made this mistake when I bought the Vendesign Machine pictured above. It does not vend gumball machines out of the box. You have to buy an extra canister that vends the gumballs, and the extra canister costs $26. Now, if I would have bought this machine brand new from the manufacturer for $400, I would be pretty upset when I put it together and it did not vend gumballs. But since I bought this machine brand new off of someone for $100, I did not mind paying another $26 to get it vend gumballs. If you bought these machines and found out that you cannot vend 1-inch gumballs, you can buy smaller gumballs and that will save you a little money.

How Much Are the Machine Parts?

This is very important and is overlooked by almost everyone starting a vending route. Before you decide what vending machine you want, you would have to take a look at how much machine parts are going to cost. For most vending machines, spare parts are cheap and reasonable, but some other vending machines are very pricey. The Vendesign Machine I use has very expensive parts. But once again, the machine is very durable so I would not worry about parts. Some people buy old, beat-up machines and then try to buy new parts to fix them up new. Be careful about this because sometimes, after you buy all of the parts to fix the machine, you might as well have bought a new vending machine.

Vending Machine Locks

Depending on what machine you decide to use, the vending machine locks might be the same as your competitors next door. Do not be alarmed. I just wanted you to be aware and keep your eyes open.

eBay

There are a lot of keys to your vending machine on eBay. Some dishonest people might buy vending keys to your particular machine and try to cash in on your hardwork. There is a very easy way to avoid getting ripped off.

Create Relationships

Let the owner of the business know that you are the only one that services the machine. If the owner sees anyone else trying to open the machine to get candy out, they would know that they are not authorized. The second thing is that you can change the vending locks and get new ones made. But that is expensive and probably not necessary. I would just not be a stranger and say hello to the owner or receptionist, or whoever you talk to when you go to service your vending machine. Just let them know you are the only one authorized to service the machine.

Stick with One Type of Machine

I see this happen all the time. People start a vending route, and they have three or four different types of machines. My advice is to pick one vending machine for your business and stick with that one. This makes it easy to keep track of your vending keys and keep your route running smoothly. You can also stock up on parts. If you have three different types of machines that you are using, then it is going to be a problem. Trust me, you are going to want to stick with one machine. Worst case scenario: two different types of machines.

"Don't worry about people stealing an idea. If it's original, you will have to ram it down their throats."

Howard Aiken

Types of Vending Machines

Like I said earlier in the book, choosing the correct vending machine for your business is the most important decision you will make. I am about to list a couple of vending machines that you might want to take a look at. Most of these machines meet most of my requirements about what makes a good vending machine.

Vendesign

Vendesign is the vending machine I use. I truly believe it is the best machine out on the market right now. These machines are very rare and hard to find.

Child-Tested

These vending machines are very tough. My 10-year-old niece Kiera tried to break one of the machines I had at home, but she failed. This machine has been child-tested. My son Jeremiah also turns the one I have at home every time he walks by and spins it as fast as he can. At first, I was mad, but I realized this was probably what was going on with all of my other machines on location, so I just kept quiet and observed. The Vendesign Machine is all metal and comes in three colors: charcoal black, yellow, and red. I say that 90% of all my vending machines are charcoal black, and you can place this machine anywhere. I have this machine at doctors and lawyers offices and pizza parlors. It really is a vending machine you can put anywhere.

Interchangeable Canisters

This machine does have interchangeable canisters, and I love that I can individually pull out each canister and change the candy. The machine also has an airtight seal which is great when it comes to preserving candy.

Coin Tube

No other machine has this, and I love it. When I first discovered the Vendesign Vending Machine, I did not know where the money was going into. I put a quarter in the machine, but I could not figure out where the money was going. After doing some research on the Internet, I found out that the money went into a tube. Each machine comes with two cash tubes. You open the machine, change the candy, pull out the tube filled with quarters, and replace it with the empty tube. I cannot tell you how easy this is. I spend three- or four-minute stop at each location. The best part is nobody sees the money. I remember the first time I changed out the coin tube. A guy was standing right next to me, watching me, and asking about vending and how to get started and what I thought about it. I was talking to him, but he did not even realize that I just took out the money and replaced it with an empty coin tube. After I closed the machine back up, he asked me what I just did. I told him I just took the money out of the machine. I had to shake the tube to let him know that money was in there. When I pulled out the tube, the coins did not even make a sound. He was impressed, of course, and so was I because before that I would have been bending down, squatting, and breaking my back to pull out the quarters from behind my old vending machines.

You Can Service This Machine Without Moving It

The next great thing about this machine is you do not have to move it. Let us say you have a Vendstar or an 1800 vending machine and it is up against the wall in an office somewhere. With those types of machines, the money compartment is in the back of the machine. You have to turn the machine at least sideways to get the money compartment. It is not that big of a deal, but it is nice that I do not have to move the Vendesign Machine at all and I do not make noise.

Very Low Maintenance

Another thing I like about the Vendesign Machine is that it is very low maintenance. I have not done any repairs on the machine. I do not carry any tools, and I do not worry about my machine breaking down.

Candy Wheel Setting

Another great value this vending machine has is the candy wheel setting. When you buy these vending machines, they have a sheet that tells you exactly what level you need to set the machine up and with what candy you are using. This information is priceless. This takes all of the guesswork out of "Am I giving away too much candy, or am I not giving away enough candy?" These machines are pretty efficient too. Once you set up the candy wheel, try putting $2 in quarters in one of the candy compartments. You will be surprised that you will probably get the same amount of candy out of the machine every time.

Coin Mechanism

Another great feature about the Vendesign Vending Machine is the coin mechanism. If you try to put anything but a quarter in the coin mechanism, it will just fall out of the side. So yes, that means when you come to your location, you will not have a penny, nickel, or dime jammed in your machine. This happened to me once before I switched to Vendesign Vending Machine. I thought I was doing well; I had all metal coin mechanisms which I thought was the way to go. When I got to the location, I was disappointed to see that there was a penny stuck in the middle coin mechanism. I tried to turn the handle and get the penny out of there, but it was jammed very badly. Long story short, I had to replace the coin mechanism because it was ruined. With a Vendesign Vending Machine, it will never happen.

How Much Does the Vendesign Vending Machine Cost?

If you buy these machines from Vendesign, they are going to cost you about $300 apiece, but they are worth every penny. You might find some deals on eBay and Craigslist. I would not pay over $150 apiece for these vending machines on these websites. I also recommend that you buy these Vendesign Machines in pretty good condition. Do not think you are going to buy these machines broken down and just buy parts because the prices of the parts will eat you alive.

Vendstar

Vendstar is the next vending machine I want to talk about. This is one of the types of machines I would consider using if I will start in vending business today. You have probably seen this machine before. It is all plastic, and it has three heads. It has three interchangeable canisters and the money drops into three individual little trays in the back that you can pull out and take the money out. My friend from high school has 300 of these machines, and this is all he does. He told me that at first, when he started out, people did not want his machines because  they looked cheap and they were breaking down. But he persevered and weathered the storm and did not give up, and now, he has a thriving business. The only downside, he says, is that he has to pay a little more attention to his route; he always carries extra parts when he goes to service his route. This machine, I believe, is a great starter machine. If you want to try out vending, buy a couple of these machines and see if you like it. You can get these machines lesser than $100 all day on eBay and Craigslist. I would not buy them from Vendstar because they charge above $200.

I Did a Little Research

Even though I said do not buy your vending machines from Vendstar, I do want to say that they are a very good company and they have been around since 1990. That might as well be a hundred years as far as vending companies go.

I Went to Their Website

I went to their site and ordered their information packet on a Monday afternoon. The next day, I had a FedEx envelope on my doorstep. I was puzzled, because I was thinking to myself I was not expecting anything. Anyway, it was Vendstar sending me their info packet; they were very thorough and had a DVD and price lists. The prices are as follows: 30 machines and candy costs $9,995, and they have a new machine called Vendstar Elite; it costs $9,995 for 20 machines plus candy. Those are just the starter packages, just so you could get an idea. Like I said before, they are good machines, but they are plastic, which might cause you problems in the long run. The new machines they make are not all plastic, but they do not have interchangeable canisters, which I believe is a must if you are going to be a vendor.

Vendstar Update

As of 2010, Vendstar has gone out of business. You can still find their vending machines everywhere, as well as parts for their machines. I would not let that stop you from using this machine, because the manufacturer in China is still selling them to distributors in the USA.

1800-Vending Machine

1800 Vending is the next machine I want to talk about. This machine has three heads and interchangeable canisters. The big difference between this machine and Vendstar is that the 1800 Vending Machine is all-metal instead of the all-plastic Vendstar Vending Machine. This type of machine can be placed virtually anywhere. They are really nice machines, and they come in a variety of colors to fit any locations.

A Couple of Downsides

The only downside I can say about these machines is that they are keyed the same for the candy compartment and the money compartment. Not a problem if you are running your own route, but in the future, if you decide to let somebody else run your route, it could cause some problems. Another concern is the metal rod that you have to push down in the middle canister to put the lid back on. Using this metal rod could be very time consuming and difficult to place back in the little hole it goes into. It takes a little getting used to, but do not let that stop you from getting this machine.

Where To Get Them

Once again, these machines are pretty popular, and you probably have seen them around. You can buy these machines too on eBay and Craigslist for around $125 or less. You can also go to their website and check them out. They are pretty straightforward, and you can talk to a representative who can give you more information. The only problem with buying directly from 1800 Vending is that they are expensive; it costs $300 and up per machine, and you ca not just buy one machine, you have to buy a package. So, if you want to build your vending route fast, I would suggest looking on eBay and Craigslist to find some good deals. This is a great machine; you cannot go wrong with this machine if you are trying to build a big route or you just want a route with no headaches.

U-Turn Vending Machine

U-Turn is another machine I want to discuss. You have probably seen this machine too. There are a couple of versions of this machine. The U-Turn, as seen here, is the original U-Turn. They also have bigger machines called the U-Turn Eliminator, the Terminator, and the Goliath.

Stick with Original First

My personal opinion is if you are going to use these machines, you might want to just stick with the original U-Turn to start. I think the other machines they make are overkill. All you need is three or four selections of candy. The Terminator and Eliminator can hold up to eight different kinds of candy, and the Goliath holds up to 12 different kinds of candy. Do not believe that just because you have 12 different kinds of candy you will make more money. All this usually means that it is going to cost you a whole lot of money to fill up this machine – maybe over $100 – and then in a couple of months, you will have stale candy that nobody wants.

Something to Think About

One thing about this machine that no other vending machine has is a slot on top of the machine for charity. This is a good place to put your charity sticker. That means someone can put money into your machine without them actually buying anything. This is great because this can cover your charity donation. I personally have never owned one of these machines, but I was e-mailing a lady in a chat room about the charity slot on their vending machine and asked how much money has she ever received from there. She told me she gets between $5.00 and $10.00 a month on some of her machines. This is a great deal because it is 100% profit; no candy was bought to get this money. This is something to think about when picking the kind of machine you will use.

Where You Can Buy Them

Once again, these machines are pretty easy to get – maybe in the $150 range on eBay and Craigslist. Like I said before, always check your local paper, eBay, and Craigslist first before you try to buy the vending machines from U-Turn. If you want a special color, U-Turn will customize a machine for you and make it just about any color you want.

Beaver Vending Machines

Beaver Vending Machines have been around since the 1960s, and I do not know why I did not decide to use them first when I started in the vending business; it would have been a lot easier. Beaver really does have the whole line of products for the vender, from bulk machines to the towers you see in movie theaters and malls. It is, hands down, the best vending company out there, and their machines have stood the test of time.

Price and Availability

With Beaver, I think that their price point is awesome. Beaver gets it: their prices are very fair. The Ball Globe Beaver Vending Machine pictured above costs $149. And that is brand new in the box. You cannot beat these prices if you are starting out in vending. Also, the second best part of Beaver is that you can find them anywhere. Just do a Google search; there are plenty of websites selling these vending machines brand new for a fair price.

All Metal

Beaver makes an excellent vending machine that is pretty much indestructible. Like the Vendesign Vending Machine, the Beaver will stand the test of time and will require very little maintenance.

Coin Mechanisms

The Beaver coin mechanisms are all metal, which is my requirement in buying a vending machine. The cool thing about the Beaver coin mechanisms is that if someone puts anything other than a quarter in your vending machine, that money will go into your money compartment. So, if some a kid drops a dime in your vending machine, it will go directly into the money compartment. I thought this was a cool and a great way to make extra money. At first, I did not think it would be a good idea, because basically, the vending machine was taking people's money. But after talking about it to a couple of people who had Beaver machines, they laughed and said they love it. One lady said she has a Beaver Machine in a pizza restaurant. She said she makes $20 every month in dimes and nickels and pennies that are dropped in her machine on top of the gumballs she sells. My mouth almost fell to the floor. She said she has not had any problems and complaints. So basically, she is getting her candy paid for at the pizza location because to the Beaver coin mechanisms.

Interchangeable Canisters

Now, I would not say Beaver has true interchangeable canisters, but you can remove the globe that holds the candy without moving the machine, and you could have an extra globe in the car and replace it. I have talked to some people who have these machines, and they say it is pretty easy; they just take the globe off and put the candy in at their car and bring it back. So, it is still fairly easy to change candy, and that is what you would want in a good vending machine.

Northwestern Vending Machines

The Northwestern Vending Machine is similar to the Beaver Vending Machine. This company has been around since 1909. Just like the Beaver Vending Machines, this company has every solution for the person that wants just one gumball machine to having a rack of machines in a mall or grocery store.

Durable Machines

Once again, these are some tough machines, and you will not have to worry about them breaking down or carrying parts with you on your route. These machines are for the professional vendor, and they will not let you down.

Price

You can get a brand new triple play vending machine at Sam's Club for $250. Do not confuse the Northwestern with the Multivend at Sam's Club. In my opinion, I do not think they are high quality, and I would not buy them. If you go to Samsclub.com, you can buy any Northwestern machine ordered and delivered to the store for pick up.

Wizard Spiral Gumball Machine

Do you really want a simple streamlined vending route? Have you ever thought about the Wizard Spiral Gumball Machine? There are a lot of imitators of this machine out there, so if you are going to buy these, remember Wizard Spiral Gumball Machine.

Very High Quality

These machines are not plastic; they are made of fiberglass. The company says "corvette quality fiberglass." I know a buddy of mine who owns 10 of these, and they are indestructible. The gumball machine also uses Beaver coin mechanisms, so you have a very-high-quality machine here. The globes are very thick and shatterproof. No tools are required for this machine.

Price

As far as prices go, these machines are not cheap; they are about $400 per one machine. It is well worth the money if you have a high-traffic location, but if you do not, then it will be hard to get your money back. It takes about four boxes of double bubble gum to fill up the machine, so you are going to want to take it into consideration as well.

A Couple of Downsides

This machine is good, but I do not believe it is for starters. The machine costs $400. Then, you are going to need another $100 the gum to fill it up, and that is not including finding a location or paying for a locator. The last thing to consider is the need for a very good location to make this work. If your gumball machine does not make $100 a month, then you are going to end up losing money.

Specialty Machines

There are a lot of vending machines popping up all the time. A couple are Buzz Bite Vending Machines, Revive Energy Machines, Dentyne Ice Vending Machines, and some Jitter Bean Vending Machines. These machines are a fad, but I would stay away from them. These machines are not in for the long haul. Maybe the Dentyne Ice Vending Machine might do well in a bar, but there are only so many bars you can target. I would advise you to just stick with what works, that is, candy and gumballs. Stay away from the machines that only serve one specialty product.

Vending Parts

If you plan on going into the vending business, you are probably going to need some extra vending machine parts. Depending on the vending machine you chose, these extra parts can get pretty expensive. The best way to handle this is to buy extra parts before you need them. There is nothing worse than when your machine breaks down, and you have to go out and buy something right away. The price is always higher.

Where to Find Parts

There are tons of websites that offer vending parts, and I will not recommend one of them. I cannot, because there are too many types of machines out there for an all-in-one site that carries everything. Do

Google searches to find companies that have parts for your particular machine.

eBay

eBay has saved me a lot of money when purchasing vending machines. eBay has also saved me a lot of money when I looked for extra vending parts for my vending machines. When looking for extra parts or vending machines, I would always check eBay and Craigslist first.

Locations

Location, location, location. We all heard these three words. As in real estate, locations for your candy machines are essential to your business. You need to know what locations work and do not work. When I first started out, if some business lets me put my vending machine in their establishment, I would have one of my candy machines there as fast as I could. Now, I am a little wiser about locations. I know what types of locations that will bring in the most money and which locations work best for me.

Random Foot Traffic

The first thing I look for in a location is random foot traffic. That means people besides the people who work in the location. If you have your bulk vending machine in a break room at a business, your only customers are the people who work there. This might work if it is a large company, but I would prefer the candy machine to be out in the lobby where anybody walking in can see it, maybe the ups man or anybody waiting there for an appointment. This is where you make the most money that impulse buys.

Captive Audience

You also want a location that has a lot of foot traffic and a place where people are waiting around. Some of the best locations I have are car wash areas. Moms are there with their kids waiting around for their car to be washed, the kids are running around and cannot be still, and the moms bribe them with some candy from my machine. I have seen it firsthand when I went to service my machines. I make a lot of money at car wash areas; I have not made less than $45 a month at a car wash location.

How Is the Business Doing?

The next thing you want to look at is whether or not the business you are thinking of locating your candy machine in is doing well itself. I remember when I first started, I had a location at a Goodyear dealership. I thought this would be an excellent location, but every time I went in there (which was usually around 11:30 in the morning), the guy at the front desk would say, "Man, you are the first person that has come in today." I thought to myself, no wonder I have never made more than $15 a month here. Nobody is buying any tires. So, you want a place that is busy, which goes back to foot traffic.

Where Is My Machine Going To Be Placed?

There are a couple of things I look for when I looking for a location for one of my candy machines. One consideration is where the machine is going to be placed. I like my machines to be placed somewhere where I do not have to ask the manager or whoever is working that day to see my machine. I once had a candy machine in a Bank of America in Riverside, California, in the company's break room. It was such a pain. I would have to talk to the manager every time I serviced the machine. Then, one of the tellers would have to escort me down to their break room and watch me service the machine. Company policy, you know. Sometimes, I would go there, and the manager would even ask me if I could come back later because they were busy and they could not escort me to the machine at the time. It was a pain doubling back on my route, and eventually, I pulled the machine out of the bank because it was getting to be a hassle.

What Time Does the Business Opens?

Another thing you might consider when looking for a location is the time the business opens and closes and what days they are open. If you have a regular five-day, 9 to 5 job, you better have your machines placed in businesses that are open on the weekend. I like locations that are open at least six days in a week and stay open to at least 7:00 p.m. This usually makes a good location. You want a location open at least six days in a week because you want the option of servicing your machine on the weekend. Also, you will make more money with your machine if it is in a business that is open at least six days or more instead of just five. I usually do not service my machines on the weekend, because I have been lucky enough to have jobs where I had a couple of days off during the week, or when I worked the night shift, I just went out and serviced the machines during the day when I woke up.

Where Is My Vending Machine?

I am going to let you know right now that when you get your machines placed at a business, sometimes, the manager or business owner likes to move them. Do not be alarmed if you go to service your machine and it is not in the same place or you do not see it in the spot where you placed it. This happens a lot, and operators I talked to get all upset when this happens. This is not a big deal. Sometimes, the business has to move your machine to put a sign or something, or if corporate people comes and wants it in a certain area. This is all part of the game. Do not be alarmed. This is why it is important to check on your machines and do not be a stranger to your location. Just remember, your machine is in their business and not the other way around, so be respectful.

+ Places to Place Your Vending Machine

1. Truck stops

2. Retirement homes

3. Nail salons

4. Clothing stores

5. Pet stores

6. Supermarkets

7. Wal-mart – yes, my buddy has one of his machines in there.

8. Airports

9. Hobby stores

10. Gyms

11. Eye care centers

12. Go-kart tracks

13. Apartment clubhouses

14. Rental manager's office

15. Secondhand stores

16. E.R. waiting rooms

17. Day care providers

18. Lawyers office

19. Banks

20. Family restaurants

21. Sandwich shops

22. Furniture stores

23. City and County buildings

24. Malls

25. Doctor's waiting rooms

26. Hair salons

27. Barbershops

28. Ice cream shops

29. Pizza parlors

30. Arcades

31. Movie theatres

32. Sporting goods stores

33. Electronic stores

34. Video game stores

35. Car dealerships

36. Boat stores

37. Marinas

38. Oil change shops

39. Pawnshops

40. Police stations

41. Fire stations – they have tours for schools all the time.

42. Smoke shops

43. Antique stores

44. Title companies

45. Escrow companies

46. Manufacturing companies

47. TV repair shops

48. Computer repair shops

49. Auto clubs

50. Drugstores

51. Laundromats

52. Print and copy shops

53. Tanning salons

54. Tattoo parlors

55. Truck stops

56. Cellular phone stores

Things to Consider

Never prejudge a potential vending location. If someone is willing to let you place your machine in their business, then I would say go for it. I will show later in this course why any location is better than your garage, and I have the numbers to prove it.

"You are never given a wish without also being given the power to make it come true. You may have to work for it however."

Richard Bach

How To Get Vending Locations

Besides choosing what vending machine to use, getting locations is the most important part of the business. There are basically three ways to get a location: doing it yourself, hiring a telemarketing locating company, or hiring what I call a door-to-door locator. I have tried all three ways to get a location. Most vendors will disagree with me when I say that hiring a locating company is the best way. For me, it is way more efficient to hire someone to find locations for you. This is your business, and you have better things to do than drive around town begging for someone to let you place your vending machines in their establishments. If you are a great salesman, then I would say go ahead and get your own locations. But if you are not, then I would recommend a vending locator.

Commission-Free Locations with a Charity

When you start getting locations for your gumball vending machines, you might be faced with paying commissions to the location. I am telling you right now, do not. You will not be in business long-splitting profits with the owner of the business you had your machine placed in. Out of all of my locations, I do not pay any commissions. I use a charity. There are numerous charities throughout the country that have what they call vending programs. Basically, you call them up and tell them that you want to be in their vending program. The charity will send you out a packet and all the information you need to fill out. You tell the charity how many gumball vending machines you have, and they will send you out that many stickers. So, say you have 10 vending machines, they will send you 10 stickers to put on your vending machines. Now, before they send those stickers out, you will usually have to agree on how much a month you will pay for each sticker. For the most part, it is usually between $1.00 and $2.00 per sticker. I pay $1.00 per sticker. For example, let us say you have 10 vending machines. You just picked the charity you will be using, and you are locating the machines yourself. You go around town and find a location. You tell the man or woman that you work with such and such charity, and you give a portion of the proceeds to them. If they say yes, you should not have to pay them any commissions, because you give a portion of the money to charities. So, everybody win. You get a location, the owner feels good because he is helping the charity by letting you put your vending machine in his or her business, the charity gets their money every month, and you pay no commissions to the location. So, all you have to pay is $1.00 per month per location. Not bad, though.

I Feel Bad; $1.00 per Sticker Is Not Enough

The charity is making great money, so do not worry about them. If a charity has 5,000 vending stickers out there, then the charity is receiving $5,000 a month on their vending program alone. So, do not think that you are scamming anybody. You are really helping the charity a lot.

Charities that Have Vending Programs

AAFLC.ORG

The American Association for Lost Children, Inc. (AAFLC) is a unique international Christian charity that actually finds and rescues missing children. It is operating strictly on donations. Vending contributions are essential to AAFLC's on-going program services of child rescues, enabling the recovery of more missing children. They offer t-shirts, brochures, and friendly support to help make your vending business a success.

AMFDC.ORG

The American Foundation for Disabled Children, Inc. is a National Charity assisting challenged children for over 15 years. They work closely with their vendors and provide everything they need to succeed.

CFOA.ORG

The Cancer Fund of America has been helping cancer pa ⌐nts and their families nationwide for over 20 years. Approximately, 91% of their net proceeds is spent on patient services.

CHILDREN-CANCER.ORG

The National Children's Cancer Society's mission is to improve the quality of life for children with cancer through financial and in-kind assistance. Their gumball vending machines program generates over $800,000 annually; 80% of N.C.C.S. income goes to help children battling cancer.

CHILDSEARCH.ORG

Project Hope is a vital source of income for Child Search Ministries; they do their best to provide vendors all they need, in support supplies, labels, and vending tips.

HUGS NOT DRUGS

Family Life International, Inc., a national 501(c) 3 nonprofit organization, with its Hugs Not Drugs and grandparents against drugs projects, seeks to end the demand for drugs by early childhood education. Their Vending Outreach Program is excellent. Visit their website to obtain a free vending start-up package.

One small note: Make sure the charity is registered in your state before you start working with them. Just let the charity representative know what state you are in, and they can let you know if they are able to help you in that state.

How To Get Vending Locations Yourself for Free

Most people in the vending industry, especially in the bulk industry, will tell you that the best way to get locations is on your own beating the doors down. If that is you, then you are in luck because I have a couple of vending scripts that will help you get your locations free without hiring a locator. If you are strapped for cash, this is a great way to get locations. When I started out in vending, I used these same scripts to find vending locations for my machines. I would suggest you memorize the script and make it your own and just tell a story. After that, a business owner will most likely let you place your vending machine in their business establishments.

Vending Locating Script 1

Hello, Mr. Prospect! I am (your name), an area representative of the (your vending charity). (Have your vending charity information and pictures in plain site at this time.) Could I please visit with you for a couple of minutes? (As your prospect looks at the pictures, tell him about the child or children from the info on the picture.) Mr.

them what your vending charity actually does.) It is my job,

representative, to get people to see these pictures and to raise fund

support the (your vending charity program.) Here is how we do it. We never ask a sponsor to donate any money. Actually, we provide a free service to sponsors. You might say we bribe your employees to make them look at our (vending charity pictures) by offering them chocolate covered raisins, smoked almonds, cashews, and other yummy treats. We place a color picture like this (show your stickers from your charity) on a vending machine like this in your break room or waiting area which allows your people to purchase these items; did I mention for only a quarter? We are totally responsible for this service. We service it. We clean it. It will never cost you a dime. I can assure you that your employees and customers will enjoy these products, because they cannot get these products from a big vending machine. If you would please consider allowing us to provide this free service, it will help us to continue to help (your vending charity.) What products do you think your people would like best? (Show them or tell them what candy you use.) Do you think you need more than one machine to start? Would your main break area be the best place to try one?

Vending Locating Script 2

Hello, my name is (your name). I am working with an organization called (your vending charity organization.) They are a nonprofit organization that helps (tell them about what your charity does and show them pictures and literature.) We are not asking for a donation; however, we are asking for a portion of your floor space on which to put this candy machine. We put pictures with an information brief of (your charity) on our free-standing machine. We have over 15 different items that we can vend in our vending machine. Would you mind helping out (your vending charity) by allowing us to provide you with a machine? We will take care of it, keep it cleaned, and maintained. There is no liability on you or your business.

Vending Locating Script 3

My name is (your name). I have a small vending business that targets a market that is neglected by most vendors. It is not a substitute for the vending you have; it is just an add-on and will vend different products than your current machine. Would you mind if I place it over in this corner, or can I put it in your break room?

I go into a business three different ways. First, with a machine and spin it while I talk to them. Second, I will show them a brochure of my vending charity. Third, sometimes I will go in with nothing. I always let them know they have no responsibility, no monthly cost, or financial obligation. I tell them I will be in once a month to service and clean the vending machine and let them know that I have a variety of candy that I can vend. This keeps the customer interested because I may swap out one or more selections that are slow movers each month. Plus, it can provide a service for their customers as well (then I will point to a place). If they say no, I will thank them for their time and then ask them to do me a favor and let me put it in for one week. If they like it, I will leave it in. If they hate it, I will come and pick it up the same day they call! (By asking this last question, I get a lot more locations.)

Use a Door-to-Door Locator with Caution

I know there are some good door-to-door locators out there, but personally, I do not have any to recommend. I have tried all three, and I have been burned by all. This is the reason why locators get such a bad name. It is my job to tell you that door-to-door locators are there, but just be careful if you decide to use them. I would go with them when they are trying to locate machines for you, if you decide to use them. Below is my horror story with them, and there are plenty more of these stories on the Internet.

My Door-to-Door Locator Story

After about four months of trying to locate myself vending machines, I got tired, and so I hired a door-to-door locating company. I finally had enough money to place my seven machines, and I was excited. After searching on the Internet a couple of months, I called a locating company. The guy seemed very professional, and he told me that he can have one of his guys out in my area in the next week. He charged me $50 a machine to locate and $50 for some administrative fees. So, I paid $400 to get my seven machines placed. I was thrilled to be getting these machines out of my garage, or so I thought. This company promised me that a locator would come to my house to pick up my machines in a van or truck and we would go find some locations. The next paragraph tells you what really went down.

The guy from the locating company called me as promised and asked me what day would be good for me. I told him Saturday was good, and he said cool, Saturday was good for him too. He told me that he would meet me at my house at 9:00 a.m. I asked him what kind of car he had. He told me he had a Toyota Corolla. I asked him, "Your boss said that you were supposed to have a van." The guy said that he did not know anything about that. I told the guy to be at my house at 9:00 a.m. and do not worry about the van since I have a van. I already spent $400 for the locating service that was supposed to provide a van or a truck to transport the machines, and they did not. So, I rented a van from enterprise rental car for $60 on Saturday for one day. I picked up the van on Friday night at 5:30 p.m. so I had to return the van at 5:30 p.m. the next day. I figured that would be enough time to locate my seven machines. Saturday came and I woke up early at 6:00 a.m., loaded up the van, and was ready to go. I had a little breakfast and watched a little TV while waiting for the locator to come to my house. 8:30 a.m. came and I got a phone call from the locator. He said he was running late. I asked him where he was. He said he was at his girlfriend's house in Pasadena, which is about 80 miles from where I was. I said okay, and he said he was on his way, and he asked me a question if his girlfriend could come along. I thought that was really unprofessional, but I did not have a problem with it, so I said okay, bring her along. I was mad but the locator said he was on his way, and he seemed very confident that he could get my vending machines placed very easily. At 10:00 a.m., there was still no sign of the locator. I gave him a call, and he told me he was still in Pasadena and there was a lot of traffic. I said okay and hung up. I gave him another hour to let him drive out a little farther, then I was going to fire him. So, I called him at 11:00 a.m. and asked him how close he was to my address. He said he was in Rancho Cucamonga, which is about 30 miles from my house. I politely told him that I did not want his services anymore. He was pissed off, and he was yelling. He asked me what kind of businessman am I. Then, that is when I got mad. I told him, "What kind of businessman are you? You did not show up on time, and you want to bring your girlfriend along." I just told him to have a good day with his girlfriend. But I lost money that day. I rented a van. What a waste. So, I took the van around town myself to try to get some machines placed, but had no luck. I called the locating company at 2:00 p.m. and talked to the owner and told him what happened. He told me he would get another locator out there as soon as possible. So, we set something up for next weekend. This time, it was an old lady. She came to pick up my machines at 11:00 p.m. on Friday. I thought that was weird, but I did not care; my machines were finally getting placed. She came in an old station wagon. When she pulled up, I was thinking, how in the hell were we going to get these machines in her car? She was very nice, a fast talker, very knowledgeable; she was giving me pointers on how to keep ants away from my machines by putting Vaseline on the bottom of the machines. She also took a quarter out of her pocket and bought a gumball on one my machines and told me it was my first sale. She was good and she told me she would have my machines placed at the end of the week. As promised, she had my machines placed within the week. She told me to meet her at a McDonald's in my area, which I did, to talk to her about the locations she got me. She gave me business cards of the places she got my machines located. She got them at a couple of pizza parlors, a mortgage company, an insurance company, a smoke shop, and a sandwich shop. She told me I had an easy route. The route was all in one shopping complex, and I thought that was cool. I asked her if I do not have to pay commissions to any locations as promised, and she said, "No, you do not have to pay any commissions." I was happy, and when I left, I shook her hand and did a drive-by of the locations. They were all there as promised, and I was really in business now. I was on a roll, or so I thought.

About three weeks went by, I figured it was time to see how my machines were doing. I first went to the pizza place, figuring this location would be profitable, and it was. There were $40 in there. I was stoked. The next place was the smoke shop; there were $20. Not bad, but the lady behind the counter asked me where her commission was. I told her the locating company told me that I did not have to pay commissions, and I told her I give money to the charity on the machine. She told me that the deal was she gets half of the money in the machine. I said okay, and I split the money with her. Of course, I was mad, but I was going to finish my route before I called the locator company. In the last five locations, I had three of the owners ask for half of the money. I was devastated. I was not going to make money in the vending business giving up half my money to my locations. I called the locating company, and nobody answered or returned my calls. A couple months later, after that, their phone was disconnected. So you live and you learn. I still kept the locations that I did not have to pay a commission, and I got rid of the locations that I had to pay a commission. My advice to you is not to use these locators that go door-to-door, who go around, and try to locate vending machines for $50 per location. They then have to split that with their boss. $25 a location with gas prices does not seem too profitable to me. These locating companies are slime balls, and I learned the hard way, so you do not have to.

Telemarketing Vending Locator

I gave up on locator companies and tried telemarketing companies. These companies charge the same amount, $50 per location, but they call businesses, and when they find you a location, they will e-mail you the location and the contact information. I have had great success with this type of location company. I have never had a problem with any of my locations, and I still have them all to this day, and I do not pay any commissions to the locations.

The Only Vending Locator I Use and Recommend

Everybody wants to know what vending machine locators I used. I have used a lot of locators, both door-to-door locators and telemarketing locators. On my website, I have said that the telemarketing locators are the type of vending locator I have had the most success with. I love how they e-mail me the location and the contact name, and I just go place my vending machine instead of wasting a weekend with a guy that finds me garbage locations.

The Company I Use Now

I have used a lot of locators, but this is the only one I will recommend because they are excellent at getting good locations that are guaranteed.

That is right. They have warranties where they will guarantee that you will at least make $20 per location. You have to know what you are doing to give this type of guarantee. Okay, I will tell you the company: it is called, Kick Start. I love these guys. They are so professional.

There Are No Minimum Orders

That is right. Kick Start is a great vending machine locator. They have the vendor in mind. Most locators will say you have to pay at least five machines to be located. Not so with Kick Start. If you only need one machine placed, no problem; just pay to have one machine placed. This is a great way to test if vending is for you. Buy a vending machine and some candy and go to Kick Start to pay for a location.

They Are Fast

This is why I recommend Kick Start instead of other vending machine locators that I have used. Once you pay, they get your locations quick. With other locators, I have waited months to get locations. Not with Kick Start; they are super fast. I paid for five machines two months ago, and two days later, I got an e-mail with the address, number, and a contact name at each locations. These guys are good, and you should give them a try if you are having trouble getting locations.

Running Your Vending Route

There is really no big secret to running a vending route, but you might have a couple of questions, so I am going to give you some simple tips to keep your vending route running smoothly and without any problems.

Dress the Part

This is a real business, and you should treat it like that. I see a lot of guys going around running routes, and they just look sloppy. They got on tank tops and flip-flops and then wonder why the lawyer does not want their vending machine in their office anymore. Of course, you do not have to wear a suit, but you should always have a t-shirt or polo shirt on from your vending charity or your own company shirt made up. Believe this goes a long way, and you will be way ahead of your competitors. It also shows that you are serious and that you will be in this business for the long run.

Dropping Off Your Vending Machine for the First Time

This might seem simple, but if you do this wrong, you could lose the location before you even start. If you are locating machines yourself, this really does not apply to you, but if you hired a locator, then it does. First, you need to introduce yourself and ask to speak to the contact person. Do not talk to anybody else, because for the most part, nobody is going to know about your vending machine. Once you get to talk to your contact person, ask the person where they would like the machine. Leave the contact person with your information. If you use a vending locator, then they will already have the information.

Servicing Your Vending Machine

Okay, you dropped off your vending machine last month, and now, it is time to service your machine. Remember to say hello or wave to your contact person or the man or woman at the front desk. They might ask you who you are. Just tell them who you are, but you should have your vending charity shirt on or your company shirt, so this should be no problem. Next, go to work and service the machine, and do it quietly. Never clean your machine with a commercial glass cleaner like Windex 409 or anything like that. This will ruin your machine, and your canisters will eventually crack. Just use plain water in a bottle, or use an organic glass cleaner like I do.

Should I Change the Candy on Location?

If you took my advice and picked one of the vending machines I recommended, then changing candy on location will be very easy and a breeze. No business wants you making noise in their office trying to pull old candy out by hand. If you have the interchangeable canisters, you can either take them off of the machine and change the candy in the car, or do what I do and have a couple of extra canisters that already have the candy in them ready to go. I carry them in a laundry basket with wheels that I bought at Wal-Mart and change the candy on location. I pull off the old candy with canisters and put on the new canisters, simple and efficient. The owners of the businesses are happy because they believe their businesses are getting fresh candy every month, even though that might not be the case; it appears that way because you are switching out the canisters every month or how often you see fit.

How To Collect Your Vending Money

This is very important, and I hope you do this. Please do not count your money while you are at a location. You do not want to draw attention to yourself. I know that on the first time you open that machine, you are going to want to see how much money you made, but please wait until you get back to your car to count your money. I am going to tell you what is going to happen if you do not do this. If you count the money while you are on location, people are going to see how much money there is in vending, and they are going to want to put a machine there, too; or, the owner is going to see, and then he or she might now want a commission. Trust me, this has happened, so please do not do it. Now, if you use Vendesign Vending Machines, the money is already collected for you in a tube. All you have to do is switch out the tube with coins and put in an empty tube. If you do not use Vendesign Vending Machines, then there is probably a money compartment in the machine. I would use a bank bag to do my collections. It is quiet and nobody can see how much money you have. These are cheap, and you can pick them up at Staples and places like that. I have also used ziplock bags when I started out, but these are clear. They work, but you have to be careful who is watching you.

Give Away Candy for Free

Yes, you heard me correct: Give away candy at every location. This is a sure way to get and keep a location. What I do after I service the location is I leave a dollar in quarters to the lady or man at the front desk or my contact person. They are happy, and then they end up putting the money back into your machine. Yes, you lose a dollar, but this goes a long way; you create a great relationship, and your location will be secure because of it.

Some More Tips on Servicing Your Machine

You should do this no matter what vending machine you have. You should always place some Vaseline at the bottom around the base of the machine. This will stop and prevent ants. I did not do this at first, but I was sorry because I got a call that there were ants allover my vending machine. It was gross, and I did not use the vending machine ever again either, and eventually I lost the location.

Best Time To Do Collections

The best time to do collections and service your machines is in the morning. I have found that 10:00 a.m. in the morning during the week is great, if you can, because by that time, most people are at work and most businesses are open. That means there will be less traffic on the streets and you can work faster. You can adjust this to fit your own schedule if you cannot service your machines during the week. I like to service them as early as possible on the weekend.

"Conquering any difficulty always gives one a secret joy, for it means pushing back a boundary-line and adding to one's liberty."

Henri Frederic Amiel

Tracking

Tracking and keeping track of your money and expenses is very important in your vending business. I have to admit that when I first started in vending, I did not do a good job of record keeping. I suggest you start at the onset of the business and do this right the first time. The easiest and cheapest way to keep track of your vending business is through a simple excel sheet. You can keep track of it all there. I tried this, but did not really keep up with it. You can also use the software that I personally use as it keeps track of everything and makes the vending business very simple.

The Tracking Software I Use and Recommend

There are a lot of vending softwares out in the market today for vending. I have tried plenty, but I only recommend one software solution. The vending software I use is Vend-Trak.

Web-Based

I love this software because it is totally web-based. I can log on any computer as long as I have my login information. This was huge for me due to the fact that last month, the hard drive on my computer failed. Luckily, my most important information, my vending business information, was safely secure at Vend-Trak.

Route Management

The second coolest thing about Vend-Trak is the route management features. I was really surprised when I entered all my addresses and information into the system. Vend-Trak has this really cool feature that optimizes your vending route based on your vending locations. I thought that I had my route optimized and nailed down. I was surprised when the system gave me an even quicker route to finish my vending route. I have over 300 machines, so this is essential to get my route done quickly.

Reports

If you love reports and data, then you need Vend-Trak. This vending software gives you so many ways to look at your data, with excel sheets and graphs and earnings by month. You can really take control of your business and see what you need to work on.

Keeping Track of Your Candy

Before I used this software, I just used to eyeball what candy I needed and estimated. With Vend-Trak, I have a complete list of all the candy I use, and I have reports on how much candy I have and what candy I need.

Keep Track of Your Mileage

Keeping track of all of your business expenses is so important. Before Vend-Trak, I would always forget to write down my mileage or accidentally throw out my mileage log. Not anymore. With Vend-Trak, I never forget, because I have to log in my collections, so it is really easy to keep track.

Coin Counter

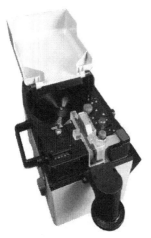

You are going to need a coin counter after you start making around $500 a month in your vending business. At first, it will be fun counting all of those quarters and packaging them by hand, but after a while, packaging quarters will become a real hassle and a job.

Packaging

The counter you chose must also be able to package your coins as well as count them. It is not good enough to have a coin counter that just counts your quarters. You need a machine that will help package your quarters without you doing them by hand. There are a lot of counters out there, so picking one can become difficult.

Counter I Use

The counter I chose to buy after some careful review was a Semacon counter. I chose this type because I can plug it in, or use the hand crank – great when my kid's package coins for me, and I do not have to worry about them plugging it into the wall. I believe my model is the s-45 (I am not sure; I bought it about 3 years ago, and it has been solid), and I have not had any problems with it. I bought it at eBay brand new for around $500. I know that was expensive, but I messed around with other cheaper counters and have been disappointed. Semacon also makes a coin sorter for a little bit more; that means, it will sort all kinds of change into different bags for you, but since I was only dealing with quarters, I decided to stick with just the counter.

Where to Find

You can get a counter anywhere; I always check out eBay first and go from there. Whatever counters you choose, I would prefer to buy a new one.

Candy

The bulk candy you use will be the third biggest choice besides the vending machine you chose and the locations you get. Most new vendors never really give the bulk candy they use, any thought, and how it affects their sales. I am telling you right now, you can have a very good location, but not even knowing it, you may use the wrong candy. Another thing you want to think about when choosing your candy is that this is your business and you make the final decision. I had a bulk vending machine at an investment company in Murrieta, California. I asked the lady at the front desk if what kind of candy she wants in the machine. She gave me a couple of suggestions, so I put the candy that she wanted in the vending machine. Every month when I came back, she wanted a different type of candy in there. So, my kindness backfired, and I lost money trying to please her with the candy she wanted. My advice to you is that you can take suggestions, but this is your business, and you make the final decision.

What Kind of Bulk Candy To Use?

This can be a mystery, or you can stick with the statistics. The best-selling bulk candy, hands down, is peanuts M&Ms. Now, wait before you leave and go to the store: if you are not careful, the M&Ms can be very messy. Imagine a hot summer day and your bulk vending machine is placed near a window. I do not care if that office has the thermostat down to 60 degrees; if that sun is beaming down on your vending machine, those M&Ms will melt, and you will lose that location quickly. When a lady in the office gets chocolate in her hands and accidentally gets it on her blouse, believe me, I know firsthand. So if you are going to use peanut M&Ms, please be careful where you put your vending machine.

My Favorite Bulk Candy: Mike and Ikes

Man, I have had a lot of success with these colorful, tasty little bad boys. If you never had any of them, I compare them to jelly beans. I love these things, and so do other people. Mike and Ikes do well in the winter and in the summer, but just like the M&Ms, please be careful where you place them in the summer.

In the summer, if your bulk vending machine is in a hot location, the Mike and Ikes will stick together and becomes one big ball. To stop this from happening, you can lightly spray the Mike and Ikes with Pam or your favorite cooking spray, and you should not have a problem in the summer time. I ignored this tip, but when I went to a couple of my locations, I was wondering why the Mike and Ikes had not moved at all since they had been a success in the previous months. After opening my vending machine, my entire Mike and Ikes were stuck together, and on the top of that the owner was complaining because people were asking for their money back, because they did not receive any candy. So please do not ignore this tip, or you could be sorry like I was at first.

Skittles

I use Skittles a lot in my bulk vending machines, and I stick with the original Skittles. Yes, there seems to be about a million different types of Skittles now, but I stick with the original type. I have tried other types, but I had the most success with the original, so I have just stuck with it over the years. I never really had any problems with this candy. It has a nice hard shell, so it does well in the winter and in the summertime.

Gumballs

Gumballs are your best friend in your business. They are, by far, the highest profitable bulk candy you can buy, and they are indestructible. The only tips I can suggest on these gumballs are to check them in your machine after a couple of months by biting into a gumball every now and then. Sometimes, these gumballs get real hard, and after that, you are going to want to get rid of them. Another thing is not to get cute with the gumballs. As with Skittles, these things come in a variety of flavors and colors. Do not get cute with buying Halloween-inspired gumballs because if you do not sell them within a month, nobody is probably going to buy them with Christmas coming around. Now, I have bought gumballs that have looked like little baseballs, and I had great success, but the baseball season is six to seven months long, so I had plenty of time to sell them. If you are just starting out, just stick with the basics until you are making money and getting comfortable with your vending route.

Bouncy Balls

How did I almost forget? These can be great. These bouncy balls never go out of style, and they never spoil or anything like that. Just be careful where you place them because little kids can choke on them. When I use the bouncy balls, I put a sticker on my machine stating "Ages 5 and Up." Most people might put three years and up, but I do not want any problems, so I put age five and up. Bouncy balls can be great; I use them at a lot of pizza places. Since at those locations there are probably vending machines other than mine that have gumballs, I use the bouncy balls.

Peanuts and Pistachios

I have used both peanuts and pistachios, and they will work if you have the right location. I have a bulk vending machine in an old folk's home in the hallway, and I cannot keep that bulk vending machine full. It is always emptying out. I use Vendesign Vending Machines, and two of the canisters hold pistachios, and the other two canisters hold regular peanuts. Those seniors love their peanuts and pistachios. I do not use any bulk candy at this particular location.

Runts, Boston Baked Beans, and Other Bulk Candy

I know there are some people who love Runts, but I have never used them. I just never really thought of Runts as a serious candy to use.

I know Runts are cheap, but every time I see a bulk vending machine with Runts, it always looks abandoned or not taken good care of. Now do not get me wrong, I know there is somebody out there that is doing well with Runts. I just do not use them. I have never used either Boston Baked Beans. I love them and buy them every now and again when I go to a gas station, but I have not tried them in my vending machines. Someone please let me know how you are doing with Runts or Boston Baked Beans so I can give a better account of these two candies, or anything else you are using that I have not mentioned on this page. Lastly, do not buy off-brand cheap bulk candy. This will just make you miserable when you walk up to your vending machine and realize you have not made any sales.

Do Not Be Cheap!

How To Store Candy

When I started out, I tried all kinds of ways to store candy. I stored candy in my house, in my freezer, in the garage, and in my closet. In the end, none of these things worked for me. I have three kids and a twin brother who lives about three miles away from me. He has two kids, and every time my brother came over, there was always some candy missing. My kids would love to open bags of candy and have Halloween in June. So, I stopped keeping candy at my house. Now, what I do is buy candy only when I need it. I go into Vend-Trak and figure out what candy I need and how much, and then, I go buy the candy. That way, I do not have all this candy around the house. This is the best way to store candy because the candy stays fresh and you have the freshest candy available.

Where to Buy Candy

The best places to buy candy, hands down, are at Costco or Sam's Club. I would not buy candy from any online store, because they charge too much. There are three other places online that I do buy candy from that you might not have thought about. These three places are Craigslist, eBay, and Amazon. Just check some of the prices. Sometimes, you can get really good deals on these sites. One time, I got four boxes of gumballs for free from Craigslist; I just had to come pick them up. The guy was fed up with the vending business. These are the best and cheapest places to buy candy. I tried contacting the companies (i.e., Craigslist, eBay, and Amazon) to buy from them directly, but I have to buy so much candy up front, and the price was not that much different than Sam's Club or Costco, so I say just buy from them.

"Try not to become a man of success, but rather try to become a man of value."

Albert Einstein

How Much Can You Make in Bulk Vending

I get this question a lot, and my answer is you can make as much as you want and as little as you want. I have 312 vending machines, and I do pretty well. Vending is a numbers game, and the more vending machines you have, no matter how well or bad the location is, you will make money. If my machines only made $10 a month, that is still over $3,000 a month gross, and that is a horrible route to my standards. I always tell people this: if you have a vending location that is making at least $10 a month, you should keep it because, if you test it with different candy, you can easily get that location up to $20 a month. The average a vending machine makes is anywhere from $8.00 to $35 a month. I would not expect more money anymore than that per machine. Do I have machines making more than $35 a month? Yes, but that is not the norm. Strive for all of your machines making at least $20 a month. I know you probably heard of machines making $100 a month and they probably exist, but those are not normal. When I talk to people trying to sell their route, and they say all their machines are making $65 a month, I know they are lying. So, like I said before, keep a location if you are making at least $10 a month and strive to get all your locations to make at least $20 a month gross profit. Below are some charts to show you how much you can make in vending.

Average $12.00 a month

Vending machines	Income per month	Total income for the year
2	$24.00	$288.00
4	$48.00	$576.00
8	$96.00	$1,152.00
16	$192.00	$2,304.00
32	$384.00	$4,608.00
64	$768.00	$9,216.00
128	$1,536.00	$18,432.00
256	$3,072.00	$36,864.00
512	$6,144.00	$73,728.00

Average $15.00 a month

Vending machines	Income per month	Total income for the year
2	$30.00	$360.00
4	$60.00	$720.00
8	$120.00	$1,440.00
16	$240.00	$2,880.00
32	$480.00	$5,760.00
64	$960.00	$11,520.00
128	$1,920.00	$23,040.00
256	$3,840.00	$46,080.00
512	$7,680.00	$92,160.00

Average $20.00 a month

Vending machines	Income per month	Total income for the year
2	$40.00	$480.00
4	$80.00	$960.00
8	$160.00	$1,920.00
16	$320.00	$3,840.00
32	$640.00	$7,680.00
64	$1,280.00	$15,360.00
128	$2,560.00	$30,720.00
256	$5,120.00	$61,440.00
512	$10,240.00	$122,880.00

Average $25.00 a month

Vending machines	Income per month	Total income for the year
2	$50.00	$600.00
4	$100.00	$1,200.00
8	$200.00	$2,400.00
16	$400.00	$4,800.00
32	$800.00	$9,600.00
64	$1,600.00	$19,200.00
128	$3,200.00	$38,400.00
256	$6,400.00	$76,800.00
512	$12,800.00	$153,600.00

Average $30.00 a month

Vending Machines	Income per Month	Total income for the year
2	$60.00	$720.00
4	$120.00	$1,440.00
8	$240.00	$2,880.00
16	$480.00	$5,760.00
32	$960.00	$11,520.00
64	$1,920.00	$23,040.00
128	$3,840.00	$46,080.00
256	$7,680.00	$92,160.00
512	$15,360.00	$184,320.00

Average $35.00 a month:

Vending Machines	Income per Month	Total income for the year
2	$70.00	$840.00
4	$140.00	$1,680.00
8	$480.00	$5,760.00
16	$960.00	$11,520.00
32	$1,920.00	$23,040.00
64	$3,840.00	$46,080.00
128	$7,680.00	$92,160.00
256	$15,360.00	$184,320.00
512	$30,720.00	$368,640.00

How To Expand Your Route by Reinvesting the Profits

I wish I would have been more committed to growing my vending business in the beginning; I would have built my little empire a lot faster than I did. I remember the first six months in business after I got my first vending machines. I was excited. I was making some decent money $400–$500 a month, and I was blowing it and not buying more machines. Almost every month, me and my buddy would go to Vegas and have fun with the money. It was not until the next year that I got serious and decided to reinvest the money in my vending business.

Reinvest Your Profits into More Vending Machines.

After my first year of vending, I had about 25 machines, and I was doing well. I was up to $500 and $600 a month, and I was happy. But I wanted to make some serious cash. So, I started reinvesting all of my profits into more machines. Every month, I would take my $500 to $600, and I would buy three or four machines. After a year, guess what happened, I had 95 machines filled with candy with locations. I was making about $3,700 gross at the time, and I was happy. So, my advice to you is that you reinvest all of your profits, and your vending route will grow very fast. I serviced out the route two days in a month. Where can you make that kind of money working for just two days in a month?

How To Set Up Your Vending Business Legally?

I left this as the last chapter because it is the least important. Most vending books start out with this information, because they really have not ran and managed route. This information applies to any business and should not be the main focus of a vending book. I am not going to bore you with corporations and all that. I will tell you this though: I have my business set up as an S Corporation. It may not be right or wrong, but that is how I have it set up. My other buddy has it set up as an LLC. Other than those two, I would not bother setting up my business any other way. There are plenty of books on which way is better, and I am not going to choose for you. Every situation is different. I will tell you this though: I used Legal Zoom, and they were great. In three days, my corporation was set up, and I got a big folder in the mail. They gave me all the information and dates about what I needed to do. They were great. They also offer on-the-phone support and e-mail support. I would not use anybody else for legal advice on setting up my business.

Vending Contracts

If you have ever tried to find locations for your bulk vending machines by yourself, you know it is hard work. Do not lose a location by trying to get the owner of the business to sign your contract. It is not worth it. Nobody is going to honor your contract anyway. If you are not keeping up with your machine and not keeping the owner happy, he or she will ask you to please remove your machine. But even if you did get him or her to sign the contract, you still can do nothing if the owner wants your machine removed. You cannot just take him or her to court.

Forget About the Contract: Handshakes Work Better

I have never used a contract to secure a location for my vending machines. It is not practical. When you get a location, the best thing you can to do to keep the location is to keep the candy fresh, show up at least once a month, and keep the owner or manager happy. If you do this, you will not need a contract.

My Story on Contracts

When I started in vending, I tried locating my vending machines by myself. I finally got a man to agree to have my vending machine in his tire shop. I was all happy and went to get my vending machine out of the car with my contract for him to sign. After I showed him the contract, he did not want the machine anymore. I told him "fine, you do not have to sign a contract." He told me forget it. I lost a location before I even started, so I say forget the contract, show him or her the charity you are with, and that is it.

"The majority of men meet with failure because of their lack of persistence in creating new plans to take the place of those which fail."

Napoleon Hill

Resources

Vending Machine Companies

http://www.vend3.com/

Richard Cuff Vendesign Manufacturing. 46 Darby Road, Paoli, PA 19301, rcuff@vendesign.com

http://www.uturnvending.com/

http://www.1800vendingtriple.com/

http://www.beavervending.com/index.asp

http://www.nwcorp.com/

My Vending Locator

Kick Start

Vending Software

Vend-Trak

All Your Legal Needs

Legal Zoom

Vendesign Manual

http://www.the-gumball-guru.com/support-files/vendesignmanual.pdf

Places to Find Candy and Machines

Usedvending.com

Ebay.com

Craigslist.com

Amazon.com

Sam's Club

Costco

Bonus

How to Buy a Vending Route?

The best way to expand your existing vending route or start a new one is to find vending routes for sale. Most of the time, you will not find vending routes for sale in the newspaper, and if you do, they are either scams, are way overpriced, or both. You have to go out and look for a route. Next time, you go out to your favorite pizza spot or sandwich shop or bank, look at the vending machines there. Is the vending machine in good shape? Is the candy stale and rotten? Eight out of 10 times, it probably is. What I do is I get the number of the vending machine and call the owner. Most of the time, the owner is tired with his or her route and wanted out.

Never Pay for What a Vending Machine is Worth!

When you are looking to start buying vending routes for sale from Craiglist, eBay, etc., you will see this line typed a lot. For example, 20 vending machines (plus the candy in the machine) and their locations are for sale, and their combined worth is $8,000; the machine and candy alone are worth $6,500. **Do not fall for this.** A vending machine is worth only what it is making in a month. I do not care if Joe paid $600 for the vending machines; he blew away $600 per machine, which is his fault.

How Do I Determine the Value of a Vending Route?

Let us use the example above. The route mentioned above has 20 vending machines. Let us say they are each bringing in $20 month after month. That is $400 a month. The experts say you should pay for a year's worth of income on a vending route. So, 400 × 12 is $4,800. That would be a fair payment for the route, but do you really know if the route is making $400 a month? No, you do not. I would offer half of that $4,800 and go from there.

Before you Write that Check!

Okay, you are excited because you found a couple of good vending routes for sale that seems to be making money and just needs a little attention. So you and the previous owner decided on $3,000. Do you get out that checkbook and write him a check for $3,000? No! You are in business to succeed. You probably cannot expand your route fast writing $3,000 checks every time you find a good route. I know I could not. You need to have the route financed, and I am not talking about getting a loan at a bank. I am talking about having the seller finance the deal. Give him 12 checks for $250; 250 × 12 = $3,000. This way, you do not have to come up with $3,000, and if the owner goes for it, you know that route will make at least the $250 a month to cover the checks you wrote.

How To Start a Vending Business?

If the owner does not go for it, the route probably does not make as much money as he or she claims to, or the owner really just might need the whole $3,000 up front. More often than not, the owner knows that the route will not make that much, and you know that this is a bad deal.

"Do what you can, with what you have, where you are."

Theodore Roosevelt

Bonus 2

Gumballs vs. Soda Machines

If you ever thought about buying gumball machines, I know you probably thought of buying those big soda and snack machines.

Well, I have thought about them too. I was really close to getting into that business. But let me tell you one thing: gumball machines are passive income; soda and snack machines are not.

If you want a job, then by all means, go and buy soda and snack machines. If you want a part-time, work-one-day-out-of-the-month, very-good-extra-income type of business, then bulk vending is for you.

I do not want to discourage you if you were thinking about going into the soda machine route, but I just want to let you know that it is not as part-time as most people think.

Bad Things About Soda and Snack Machines

1. You have to service your machines at least once a week.
2. You will need a truck or van to transport your machines.
3. It is very expensive to start; a good used machine will cost $1,000.
4. You will lose a lot of money if you do not know what you are doing.

5. These machines require maintenance; they do not run on autopilot.

6. You will get complaints and phone calls from your customers.

7. Did you think about keeping the machine stocked with change? If you do not do it, you will lose money.

8. Think about your exit strategy: if you wanted to quit the business today, how hard would it be to get out?

9. It takes a long time to service the machines.

Good Things About Soda and Snack Machines

1. Good income. Four figures a month after you get things going.

2. This could be your only job if you build your business up.

3. Once your machine is on location, you are in business.

4. You can really make some good money.

Bad Things About Gumball Machines

1. You will need a lot of machines to match soda and snack income.

2. Family and friends will laugh at you, until you start bringing in cash.

3. You will not be able to quit your job with 20 machines.

Good Things About Gumball Machines

1. It only takes one day a month to service machines.

2. Any car will transport a bulk vending machine.

3. It is cheap to start. I have bought new machines for $50 before.

4. It is very hard to lose money even if you have no clue.

5. These machines will run on autopilot.

   No complaints, no calls.

6. The machine only takes quarters, so there is no problem.

7. I could easily get out of the business if I wanted to.

8. Only four minutes or under is needed to service each machine.

"The rung of a ladder was never meant to rest upon, but only to hold a man's foot long enough to enable him to put the other somewhat higher."

Thomas Henry Huxley

Made in the USA
Las Vegas, NV
07 March 2021

19154718R00074